LeGEND

 INTRODUCING THE TOPIC    DISCUSSING WITH THE GROUP

 EXPLORING CREATIVELY   STUDYING THE SCRIPTURE

 STORYTELLING   REFLECTION

 ROLEPLAY    SMALL GROUP OR PAIRED DISCUSSION

Dedicated to the memory of Lanny Chandler, whose enthusiasm, humor and faith inspired a generation of young people.

Living the Good News, Inc.
a division of The Morehouse Publishing Group
Editorial Offices
600 Grant Street, Suite 400
Denver, CO 80203

Cover Design and Layout: Val Price
Photography: Marc Dickey, Regan MacStravic, Ann Addison

Printed in the United States of America.

The scripture-based activities contained herein have been created using the Today's English Version, © 1992, American Bible Society. Used by permission.

ISBN 1-889108-06-5

QuickTakes for teens

Easy, on-the-spot Resources for Youth ministry

volume 4

relationship ISSUES

Dirk deVries

INTRODUCTION

For me it started in Denver in the early 1980's. I was—finally—a youth pastor! A teen beacon, a shepherd to the oddly-shorn sheep, a hip-hop, happenin', cool guide through the rocky crags of adolescence into the grateful, fruitful plains of adulthood. It was my calling, my mission, my vision.

"Didn't you know," someone cheerfully asked, "that the average youth pastor only lasts eighteen months?" *Eighteen months?* What kind of legacy can I leave in eighteen months? I expected to be doing this at least along enough to receive two generations' worth of nice thank-you notes.

But no, according to the stats—back then anyway—most of us could only stand eighteen months of...

- sleepless weekend retreats where—due to either a planning glitch or our own innocent inexperience—we not only led all the sessions, all the games and all the rites, but also stayed awake all night saying "Quiet down!" "Get back in your room!" and "I mean it this time!"
- pacifying the custodian who demanded to know who stuck the pizza (pepperoni and mushroom) to the ceiling of the fellowship hall
- listening to the teen who just...got dumped by his girlfriend...learned her parents are divorcing...got rejected from the college she'd dreamed of attending...lost his place on the soccer team

I lasted five and a half years, proud, I might point out, to have gone four years beyond the average. But I couldn't really give it up; there's something that gets under your skin...or under mine, anyway. And if you are reading this book, you share this desire to make God's grace real for teens. Whether full-time or for ninety minutes a week, you are a "youth minister."

And you are very busy.

And so we designed this book for you.

No, not more session plans. Just tons of proven, practical, creative activities from which to pick and choose...
- to fill in an already prepared but incomplete meeting
- to supplement a catechetical session when some topic demands immediate attention
- to open or close a meeting
- to fill an extra 15-20 minutes you didn't expect to have

It's a wild smorgasbord of opportunities for your group.

This book also acknowledges that no two groups are the same. Your group is unique. No other group faces the same mix of issues, with the same time constraints, the same interests and the same abilities. An a la carte menu of possibilities makes

(continued on next page)

sense—prayers, discussions starters, art, drama and music choices. You choose what your experience and intuition tell you will work the best.

I encourage you to browse through the book before the need for it arises. Get a feel for the broad topic areas so that, when you need an activity or a discussion starter, you'll already know where to look and what's available. Flag ideas that strike you as particularly useful for your group.

Bolded words key you in immediately to needed materials or required preparation. Easy-to-find symbols throughout the book help fit activity styles to your needs.

LeGEND

 INTRODUCING THE TOPIC   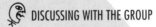 DISCUSSING WITH THE GROUP

 EXPLORING CREATIVELY   STUDYING THE SCRIPTURE

 STORYTELLING   REFLECTION

 ROLEPLAY    SMALL GROUP OR PAIRED DISCUSSION

ToPiCS

Here's a quick run-down of the topics in this volume of Quick Takes:

- *Prejudice and Racism:* Use the suggestions found here to explore the roots and dangers of prejudice and racism. Several activities help group members experience points of view other than their own. Other topics covered include sexism, ageism, scapegoating and cliques.
- *Peer Pressures:* This section offers creative ways to examine a number of activities that teens feel pressured to take part in, including drug and alcohol use, gangs and foul language. A number of activities specifically explore addiction and the desire to be "popular" and fit in.
- *Moral Choices:* Here, activities offer ways to guide teens in making everyday tough choices, involving lying, gossiping, sex, cheating and stealing. Group members are given the opportunity to identify their struggles and to come up with their own solutions.
- *Friendship Skills:* In this section, you'll discover ways to help group members sharpen their people-helping skills, like listening, confronting and supporting. We also offer activities that explore dating and the complexities of relationships.
- *Loneliness and Jealousy:* This section examines both of these painful "relational" emotions, looking at their causes and ways to cope and grow beyond them.

We hope you have fun and find meaning with the members of your group using the ideas presented in Quick Takes, Volume 4.

TiPS

■ Avoid praising kids for what they do, which encourages them to accept themselves based on what they do, not who they are. Instead offer "unconditional love," affirming and encouraging them as God does, simply for being God's children.

■ Kids tend to fixate on personal appearance. Like all of us, they want to fit in, appear normal and find acceptance. Help them talk about their fears. Discuss media stereotypes and encourage self-acceptance.

■ You and the kids don't have to agree on values. They are, however, interested to know what you believe and why. Don't hesitate to share your values, and always listen respectfully to theirs.

■ Younger adolescents are working toward:
   — establishing an independent self-identity
   — discovering emotional stability
   — finding honesty, clarity, transparency...people they can trust
   — exploring the new need for closeness and intimacy
   — finding healthy outlets for incredible physical energy

■ Older adolescents are working toward:
   — discovering that they are "okay" as they are, even when differing from others
   — developing strong and positive friendships, especially outside the home
   — knowing the world as it really is, good and bad, pleasurable and painful
   — practicing new-found maturity, including decision-making
   — finding unconditional love

■ Every kid is unique. Each views the world differently and processes information in his or her own way. This is a humbling truth for those of us who lead. The way *we* see and experience the world is unique to *us*, and may not be shared by them. How will we acknowledge and allow for these differences?

ICeBREaKeRS
DReSS 'EM UP

Divide participants into smaller groups of 4-5 members each. Give each group a stack of **old newspapers**, a roll of **masking tape** and a pair of **scissors**. Offer these directions:

■ You have 15 minutes to "dress" a member of your group in newspaper.
■ Make your newspaper outfit as outlandish and wild as possible.
■ The most creative group wins.

Let groups work to create newspaper costumes for a member of their group.

Note: Be aware that the ink will come off the newspaper, so whoever is being "dressed" needs to be wearing old, washable clothing. Instead of newspapers, you can use newsprint (which will be much cleaner, but more expensive), stacks of tissue paper (which is flimsier and tends to tear easily) or butcher paper (which is stiffer and harder to work with).

PaRTY GAMeS

Any of a number of popular party games make good ice breakers for teens. You can always put a relevant spin on a game by picking up on the focus of the meeting. Here are several examples:

- Charades (A meeting dealing with the impact of television could begin with a game of Charades that use only TV-show titles.)
- Picture Charades (A meeting dealing with world concerns could begin with a game of Picture Charades that cover concepts like hunger or religious oppression.)
- Twenty Questions (A meeting dealing with friendship could begin with a game of Twenty Questions that ask about famous friendships in the Bible, like David and Jonathan or Ruth and Naomi.)

FiNDiNG GoD

Invite each group member to complete one of these incomplete statements:

- Today, I found God in...
- Today, I saw God when...
- Today, I was aware of God when...
- Today, I felt the presence of God as...

Continue the activity as long as members continue to offer completions.

SCuLPT iT

Distribute one of any number of **sculpting media**, for example, modeling clay, pipe cleaners, foil, etc. Invite each group member to sculpt something related to the focus of the meeting, for example:

- a hope for the group
- a personal fear
- a contribution you can make to the group
- a wish for the world
- an item in your life, 20 years from now
- your favorite pastime
- your greatest talent

Invite volunteers to show and explain their completed sculptures to the group.

ReDO THE DaY

Invite group members to take turns completing this statement:

- If I could redo today, the one thing I'd do differently is...

Tips & Icebreakers

PREJUDICE & RACISM

Prejudice & Racism

ANiMAL STeREoTYPeS

Divide the group into 3-5 smaller groups. Assign a different animal identity to each group. Ask each group to make its own animal name tags using **index cards, markers** and **pins**. Then give each group **paper** and **pencils** with these directions: Each group represents a different species. Each species would rather not associate with animals of other, inferior species. List the reasons why you don't want to be around the other animal groups. Explain why your species is the best and why the others are inferior.

After 10 minutes, reconvene and ask group members to discuss, in character, their lists. Then ask:

■ How did you feel as you listened to the other groups speak about you and your group?

■ How did you decide what to criticize about the other groups?

■ How did you decide what to brag about in your own group?

LaY iT DoWN

Ask group members to stand in a circle and to offer prayers about prejudice by finishing these sentences:

- Lord, today I lay down my feelings of prejudice about...
- Lord, thank you for showing me...

RaCiSM ALeRT

Ask group members to discuss:

- Define *racism*. (You may wish to provide **dictionaries** and to select the definition most meaningful to group members.) Compare *racism* to *prejudice*, *bigotry* and *discrimination*.
- Why is racism evil? What does it do to people? to self-esteem? to love?
- Why does racism exist? What does it do to those who are racist?
- What do you think Jesus would do about racism?
- What races are represented in our society? our community? our church?
- Who among us has experienced first-hand the effects of racism? How does it feel? What does it look like?
- Where do you think racism exists in our society? in our community? in our church? in our school?
- How can we fight racism as individuals? as a class? as a church? (List answers on **chalkboard or newsprint**.)

HiSTORY OF PReJUDiCE

Begin with the activity Accepting Our Differences (p.10). Then invite each group member to remove one article or picture from the table. Distribute **paper** and **pencils** and offer these directions:

- Spend a few minutes writing about the conflict in your picture or article. Write from the point of view of each of the sides involved in the conflict.
- Describe what you are feeling and why you are fighting. Tell your side of the story.
- Try to enter the mind and heart of *both* of the parties in conflict, giving voice to their hurt, anger, frustration, confusion and fear.

After several minutes, ask volunteers to share what they have written. If time allows, repeat the activity, using conflict situations from group members' schools, workplaces or neighborhoods in place of national or international conflict.

ACCePTiNG OuR DiFFeReNCES

Distribute **scissors** and **recent copies of news magazines and newspapers**. Ask group members to cut out articles and pictures reporting people in conflict. Gather the group and spread the pictures and articles on a table. Ask each group member to report on one of the items he or she cut out. Discuss:

■ Over what differences are all these people in conflict?

■ What differences seem small to us? large?

■ How do you think God feels about these differences?

LoViNG THE ENeMY

Distribute **paper** and **pencils**. Ask each group member to write down the names of:

■ One person you consider to be your enemy.

■ One religious, political or national group you consider to be your enemy.

Discuss:

■ What is an enemy? Why do we consider others our enemies?

■ Why do you think Jesus commands us to love our enemies (Lk. 6:27)?

■ What specific actions do people use to show love to children? parents? friends? spouses? teachers? the sick or lonely?

■ In what ways can each of these specific actions be extended toward those we consider our enemies?

■ What turns enemies into friends?

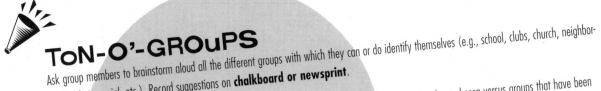

ToN-O'-GRouPS

Ask group members to brainstorm aloud all the different groups with which they can or do identify themselves (e.g., school, clubs, church, neighborhood, ethnic, social, etc.). Record suggestions on **chalkboard or newsprint**.

Then divide into smaller groups of 3-5 members. Ask these small groups to talk about the groups they have chosen versus groups that have been thrust upon them by birth, parental direction, etc. Also ask them to identify other groups that they fear, dislike or don't understand. Remind group members to speak with respect.

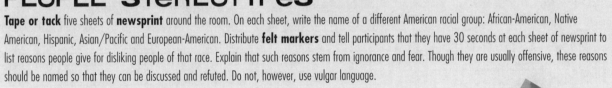

PEoPLE STeREoTYPeS

Tape or tack five sheets of **newsprint** around the room. On each sheet, write the name of a different American racial group: African-American, Native American, Hispanic, Asian/Pacific and European-American. Distribute **felt markers** and tell participants that they have 30 seconds at each sheet of newsprint to list reasons people give for disliking people of that race. Explain that such reasons stem from ignorance and fear. Though they are usually offensive, these reasons should be named so that they can be discussed and refuted. Do not, however, use vulgar language.

Call time every 30 seconds until all group members have had time at every list. Then read the lists aloud and ask:

- How did you feel as you listened to what was written on the list for your racial group?
- Where did you get the ideas you listed on the sheets? What did you feel as you wrote them?
- How did you decide what to write on the list for your racial group?
- In what ways do we see racial prejudice demonstrated?
- What can we do to stop ourselves from stereotyping people of other races?

Continue with the activity Racism or Salvation (p. 2).

RACiSM OR SaLVATiON

First complete the activity People Stereotypes (p.11). Then distribute **Bibles** and read aloud Romans 13:8-11. Invite group members to describe a real-life situation involving racial prejudice that they have experienced or witnessed. Ask:

■ How would that situation have been different if those involved had followed Paul's guidelines?

■ In what ways is racism like sleep? What kind of wakefulness do we reject when we deal in stereotypes?

Take the group outside to burn the five lists of stereotypes. As each list burns, group members could repeat a simple litany: *Loving God, let your love burn away prejudice.*

NoT SO DiFFEReNT

Ask group members to choose partners to discuss:

■ How are we different? Name different perspectives, experiences, choices, etc.

■ What do we have in common? What makes us similar? Name similar interests, traits, hopes, problems and feelings.

Bring the group together again and invite members to call out similarities and differences that they discovered. List these on **chalkboard or newsprint** in two columns. Then ask group members to identify which similarities and which differences are really significant. Circle these and invite discussion.

ACCUSaTiON MeDiTATiON

Begin with the activity Scapegoating: You Did It! on page 14. Invite group members to stand together in a circle, close their eyes and respond *in silence* as you lead them through the following meditation:

■ Whom are you blaming *right now* for something for which *you* are responsible? a parent? a friend? a teacher? God? society? a certain ethnic group? *(Pause.)*

■ What can you do *this week* to take responsibility for that for which you've been blaming someone else? *(Pause.)*

■ What can you do *this week* to make a change in this area? *(Pause.)*

Close by praying: God, sometimes it's hard to look at ourselves and say, "It's our fault." We feel better blaming others; then we feel better about ourselves and we don't have to work to make changes. Make us responsible, in Jesus' name. *Amen.*

GROUPS: GOOD AND BAD

Divide **chalkboard or newsprint** into two columns. Label one column *Pros* and the other *Cons*. Ask:

- What are the pros and cons of having groups to which you belong?
- What are the positives and what are the negatives of having boundaries between groups?
- When have we experienced being inside a group? When have we experienced being outside a gorup?
- How can we understand the power of "be-longingness" without succumbing to the hurt-fulness of exclusivity?

CUTTING CLIQUES

The early Church also suffered from cliques—groups that feared, suspected and excluded others. Distribute **Bibles** and ask a volunteer to read aloud 1 Corinthians 1:10-17. Ask:

- What was dividing the believers?
- How did Paul feel about these cliques?
- What is Paul's advice?
- What has been lost because of the divisions?
- What divides people at your school? in your neighborhood or city? in your church?
- What is lost because of these divisions?
- Paraphrase Paul's argument by substituting one of the factors that divides students at your school. *Example:* "One says, 'I'm a freshman'; another, 'I'm a senior.' Education has been divided into groups! But aren't we all there for the same purpose?"

SCaPEGoATiNG: YoU DiD iT!

Begin by accusing someone in the group of having done something. (When choosing the *accused*, try to select someone in the group who can respond creatively.) You can make up what this person supposedly "has done"; let the accusation be humorous. Here are some possibilities:

- You beat my prize fish—the one I really loved a lot—against the wall. Now it's dead! YOU DID IT!
- You broke my lava lamp! YOU DID IT!

Let the *accused* defend him- or herself, as wildly and creatively as possible. You might offer examples of defenses, such as:

- I couldn't possibly have done that...it wasn't me...I *love* fish...in fact, my mother is a fish...*lots* of my relatives on my mother's side are fish...I couldn't possibly kill a fish...

The *accused* then ends his or her defense by accusing another member of the group, including saying why it was likely this new *accused* did it:

- *John* did it, yes, that's right, John did it because a fish once, um, once mistreated him, back when he was five years old and very impressionable ...yes, that's it...

Continue until several group members have offered defenses and accusation (or longer, if members are enjoying the activity). Follow up the activity with the Accusation Meditation on page 12.

SeEiNG INSiDE

Distribute **Bibles** and ask a volunteer to read aloud 1 Samuel 16:1-13. Ask:

- Why were David's brothers more likely candidates for king?
- What made David last on the list of possibilities?
- What assumptions might Samuel and Jesse have been making about David?
- How do you think David felt when he saw his father's reluctance?
- What did God teach Samuel and Jesse through this?
- When have you been judged, ignored or rejected because of what someone assumed about you?
- On what basis do we judge our peers? our neighbors?
- What traits or behaviors keep us from getting to know others?
- How can we guard against judging others on the basis of things that don't really matter?

14

SoMeONE ELSe'S SKiN

Distribute **paper** and **pencils**. Invite participants to reflect silently about the human characteristics or traits that become the basis for other peoples' prejudices. Ask group members to write a prayer for someone who has been rejected because of prejudice. Then gather in a circle and invite volunteers to read aloud their prayers.

TO aN UNKNoWN GOD

Distribute **Bibles** and get into groups of four or five members. Ask small groups to read Acts 17:22-34 and discuss:

- ■ How does Paul show respect for the religious beliefs of the Athenians?
- ■ What is good about the way Paul talks to the people about God? How else might he have handled it?
- ■ How can we show respect for the religious beliefs of others? What can we learn from Paul about talking to people about our faith?
- ■ What makes Christianity unique?

SeXiSM

Ask group members to define the word *sexism*. If they need help, suggest: *Sexism is the unfair treatment of people because they are female or because they are male.*

Invite group members to suggest examples of sexism as a volunteer lists their examples on **chalkboard or newsprint**. Discuss:

- ■ When have we been the object of sexism? How did we feel at these times? How did we handle it?
- ■ Why is sexism destructive? What affect does sexism have on people's self-image? on their opportunities to use their gifts?
- ■ What is the purpose of sexism? What does sexism try to protect? to achieve?
- ■ Where might we be guilty of sexism in our church? our group? our schools? our homes?
- ■ How do you think God feels about sexism? What might God be asking us to do about sexism?

AGEiSTS ANoNYMOuS

Before the meeting invite two or more elderly members of your parish to join your group for this discussion. Ask these **guests** to prepare a few remarks about aging, for example:

■ What has surprised you about aging?
■ What are the special benefits of age? special challenges?

In your meeting, distribute **construction paper** and **markers** and ask all participants to create name tags for themselves that include two or three small drawings that reflect their special interests. Then go around the circle introducing yourselves, explaining the drawings on the tags. Ask the senior guests to share their observations about aging, prepared beforehand.

AGEiSM: BuT WHaT ABOuT..?

Begin with the activity Ageists Anonymous. Then open the meeting for questions. Invite group members to ask any question of the guests. *Suggestions:*

■ Was it a shock to grow old?
■ When did you notice you were older?
■ How do you regard your teenage years? Do they seem far away or close? How relevant to your life do they seem now?
■ How is the world different from when you were a teen?
■ Do you like the life you've led? Do you like the life you're leading now?
■ How important is your faith to you? How big a part of your life is God? How has your relationship to God changed?
■ What are the toughest lessons you've learned in life?
■ How have your values changed as you've grown?

AGEiSM: BLESSiNG aND PRAYeR

If you invited senior guests to your meeting, invite them to stand in the middle of the group circle. Ask group members to come together around the guests, placing their hands on the guests' heads and shoulders. Ask group members to repeat each phrase of this blessing after you (Pause after each line):

> Loving and protective God,
> grant these your children
> opportunities to share their wisdom
> and delight in the world's beauty.
> Amen.

Switch roles, asking group members to stand together in a tight circle as the senior guests stand around them and repeat the same blessing.

AGEiSM: SiMEoN aND ANNa

Distribute **Bibles** and ask a volunteer to read aloud Luke 2:21-35. Discuss:

- This passage tells of an important "growing up" event in Jesus' life. Why is he in Jerusalem with his parents?
- What clues in this passage suggest that Simeon is an older man?
- In your own words, what does Simeon predict about Jesus? What will Jesus do? Who will Jesus be?
- In what ways do Simeon's words about Jesus come true?

Ask a volunteer to read aloud verses 36-38. Discuss:
- Who is Anna?
- In your own words, what does Anna predict about Jesus? According to Anna, what will Jesus do?
- In what ways do Anna's words about Jesus come true?
- In our church, what "prophetic words" do the elderly bring? How do our elderly Christians, like Simeon and Anna, help us to understand who Jesus is? what God asks of us? how much God loves us? what part we play in God's plan?
- How can we make sure we hear the "Simeons" and "Annas" in our lives?

PEER PRESSURES

Peer Pressures

IF YoU WeRE ADDiCTED

Before your meeting, secretly invite two or three volunteers to take the parts of teenagers struggling with alcohol and drug use. Ask each volunteer to think of a brief "story" about his or her addiction to present to the group.

Examples:
■ My dad drinks a lot, so he never notices when booze is missing at home. It's easy for me to drink at night when I'm home alone. But now it's like I can't stop.

■ My friends and I smoke dope. It's no big deal. I'm not really addicted, I just like it. Sure, my school work suffers, but dope is more fun than school anyway.

Seat the volunteers before the group and invite the volunteers to explain their "problems" to the group. Then ask: What advice would we suggest to help these friends? The only requirement for our advice is that it has to be really *bad* advice. Invite group members to offer their bad advice. (*Examples*: Don't worry about it. It's just a phase; you'll grow out of it. What's wrong with you? Why can't you just stop? C'mon, grow up!)

INTOXICATION

Before the meeting copy each of the directions below on a separate **slip of paper**. Add others if you wish. Prepare one slip per group member. Place the slips in a **basket**.

Directions: talk too loud; talk slowly and deliberately; slur your speech; blur your vision by squinting; stare blankly at people; tell each person that he or she is your best friend; describe things around you as more intense; pretend to be a bird; act depressed; be afraid; shake; stumble; convulse; spin in a circle; cry; sing nonsense; stand too close to people; fall asleep; talk about yourself; etc.

In the meeting, invite each group member to draw one slip from the basket. Give these instructions: Each slip has an instruction written on it. Keep your instruction secret. For the next 5 minutes, interact with the other people in the room following the instruction written on your slip.

Observe what happens, and then discuss:

- What was happening? What do you think this activity is trying to illustrate?
- What behaviors did you find most annoying? most hurtful? most frustrating?
- Imagine yourself in a store or a classroom when someone exhibits these behaviors. How do people respond? How do you respond?
- When have you witnessed these behaviors as a result of someone else's drug or alcohol use?
- When have you experienced these symptoms because of your own drug or alcohol use?

DRuGS AND DeSPAiR

#1 Alcohol is the most widely used drug in the world.

#2 Abusing drugs can affect a person's breathing and cause confused thinking, nervousness, fear, organ damage, nausea and seizures.

#3 Withdrawing from drugs causes sweating, shaking, chills, sickness, stomach pain and leg cramps.

#4 You can quickly become addicted to alcohol and other drugs.

#5 Using alcohol or other drugs for pleasure or to fit in, relax or escape problems can dull thinking, harm the body and allow a person to make bad decisions. Anybody can become an addict.

DRuGS: HOoKeD

Place **a bowl of Skittles® or M&Ms®** on the table. Invite volunteers to come forward, one at a time, to take *one* candy from the bowl. When all who wish to come forward have done so, invite anyone who would like one more candy to come forward for one additional candy.

Observe members' responses as they come forward. Do some take more than one? Are some trying to sneak more? What comments do they make about the candies? about only being allowed to take *one* of the candies?

Allow people to come forward a third time for just one more of the candies, then discuss:

■ Who would really like to come up and take more Skittles®?
■ Why are these candies so "addictive"? What do we mean when we say that?
■ What about Skittles® is so appealing? the flavor? texture? color? size?
■ Describe your craving for Skittles®.
■ Now imagine that you are addicted to these candies. You've *got* to have them. What is the sordid end of your obsession with Skittles®?

Record group members' answers to this final question on **chalkboard or newsprint**. Encourage extreme, creative and humorous answers; for example:

■ You salivate when you hear the word Skittles®.
■ You're caught stealing money from your mother's wallet to support your habit.
■ Your friends start avoiding you because all you talk about is this candy and they don't like your Skittles® breath.
■ Your hair falls out because you eat these candies constantly and no longer eat healthy foods.

Note: Definitions of addiction vary. These activities operate with this definition: Addiction is the use of a substance, belief or behavior to avoid responsibility and anesthetize against painful feelings. Write this definition on **chalkboard or newsprint**. In these activities, group members will be encouraged to think of addiction broadly, identifying not only obvious addictions, like those to alcohol, drugs or tobacco, but also more subtle forms of addiction, like those to religious beliefs or behaviors, food, sex, other people or exercise.

LiViNG CaREFuLLY

Distribute **Bibles** and ask a volunteer to read aloud Ephesians 5:15. Discuss:

- Give drug- or alcohol-related examples of
  — "being careful how you live"
  — "living like ignorant people"
  — "living like wise people"

Ask a volunteer to read aloud Ephesians 5:16. Discuss:

- What do you think the author of Ephesians means by, "These are evil days"? What kinds of "evil days" do we see in our culture?
- In what ways can drugs and alcohol keep us from "making good use of every opportunity"? What opportunities can be missed because of drugs or alcohol?

Ask a volunteer to read aloud Ephesians 5:17. Discuss:

- What alternative to abusing alcohol does the author suggest?
- What do you think it means to be "filled with the Spirit"? Practically speaking, how do we accomplish this?

THe FUTuRe YoU

After reviewing the information in Drug and Despair (p. 19), distribute **paper** and **pencils** and invite group members to reflect silently on the following: Pick a drug. Pick alcohol, cigarettes, marijuana, speed, coke, crack, acid, angel dust, smack...whatever drug you want. Pick a drug you know something about and write it down. Now project yourself into the future. You're a regular user, abuser and misuser of the drug you've picked. Ten years pass... Twenty years pass... How old are you now?

Then ask the following questions, pausing briefly after each question to allow group members to write their responses:

- Knowing what this drug can do to you, describe yourself 20 years from now.
- How much has your drug use cost you?
- What's your physical condition?
- What's been the effect on the people who know and care about you?
- What's happened to your mind?
- What kind of job—if any—have you managed to keep?
- What's the next 10 years of your life look like?

Volunteers may wish to share their reflections with the group.

A BeTTER FuTuRE

Begin with the activity The Future You (p. 21). Then ask group members to stand in a circle. Explain: Your future *without* drugs stretches before you...20, 30, 40, 50 or more years. Imagine yourself at 50, drug-free, strong, healthy, satisfied, enjoying life. What are you doing at 50 that you still love to do and do really well? Invite each person to give one brief answer to this question. (*Examples*: running 5 miles a day, singing in a rock group, traveling around the world with the money I haven't spent on drugs, etc.)

Close by asking group members to reflect in silence for 1 minute on this question: *Why do drugs?*

IN oR OuT?

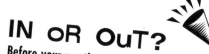

Before your meeting pick some superficial criterion on which group members will be judged to be "in" or "out." Possible choices include:

- people wearing neck jewelry are "in"; people not wearing neck jewelry are "out"
- people wearing sneakers are "in"; people wearing any other kind of footwear are "out"
- people wearing T-shirts are "in"; people wearing other kinds of shirts are "out"

Avoid choosing as your criterion a physical characteristic or a characteristic that separates people by race or socio-economic status. *Do not* share your chosen criterion with the group. As participants arrive, identify "in" people and give them some kind of **snack**. As "in" people enjoy the food, invite the group to figure out what the "in" people have in common.

REaLiTY CHeCK

Divide into groups of two or three. Ask the following questions, pausing as needed to allow time for discussion:

- If you were hooked, what would you need (or want) to hear from a friend? What could they say or do to start you toward getting "unhooked"?
- What would be the *wrong* thing for a friend to say to you or do for you? What would you definitely *not* want them to say or do?
- When have you tried to help a friend who was struggling with substance abuse? What was the result? What helped? What didn't help? What did you learn?
- As a group, come up with three suggestions for someone trying to help an addicted friend.

Gather participants and invite volunteers from each group to share their best ideas and insights. Ask:

- How do we know when a situation is beyond our ability to help?
- When it's beyond our ability to help, to whom do we turn?

MaKiNG CHOiCeS

Ask each group member to find a partner. Give the following instructions:

■ With your partner, summarize in one or two sentences the attraction of drugs and alcohol.

■ But drugs and alcohol, though in many ways attractive, also come with a potentially heavy price. What price do we pay for abusing drugs and alcohol?

After several minutes, ask partners to change the focus of their discussion:

■ With your partner, talk about how you make decisions in life. At first, don't talk about drugs; instead, talk about a simple decision, like which movie to see with a friend or what to order at a restaurant. How do you make these decisions?

Give partners 3-4 minutes, then continue:

■ Now switch back to the subject of drugs and alcohol. You're at a party with some new friends and someone offers you a selection of pills. "Have one," she says. "Go ahead, try it."

■ With your partner, decide how you make this decision.

Give 5 more minutes, gather group members and discuss:

■ What's involved in making decisions about using drugs and alcohol? What part do each of the following play:

— the law
— peer pressure
— God and faith
— respect for others
— self-esteem
— fear of consequences
— your hopes for your future
— knowledge of the dangers
— stress

FoUL BaLL

This discussion challenges teenagers to consider the effect foul language has on others. Start the activity by writing these words on **chalkboard or newsprint**: swearing, profanity, cursing, foul language, obscene language. Ask:

■ What do each of these mean? (A **dictionary** may be helpful at this point.) What do they have in common? How are they different?

■ Why do people use foul language? What "rewards" do we get for foul language? How does foul language gain us respect? action? attention? revenge?

23

PLuS aND MiNUS

Post a large sheet of **newsprint** on the wall. Divide it into two columns, labeling one with a large plus sign (+), and the other with a large minus sign (-). Then invite group members to name both positive and negative aspects of belonging to a gang. Record ideas in the appropriate columns. When group members have completed the list, point to the last two people to have spoken and say, "Bang! You're dead." These two group members join the previous casualties in the "dead zone." (See activity Bang! You're Dead, below.) Then ask:

■ What needs does gang membership fill for gang members? In what other ways could these needs be met?

GaNG FoLLY

Distribute **Bibles** and ask a group member to read aloud Genesis 37:12-34. Then ask:

■ What aspects of gang life do we see in Reuben and his brothers?

■ What motivates the brothers' efforts to kill Joseph? When have you heard of gangs dealing with their members in the same way?

■ What makes a person do something in a group that he or she wouldn't do alone?

■ What motivates Reuben's desire to save Joseph? What risks does he take in going against the other brothers?

■ What effect do the brothers' actions have on their father? How does this reflect the reality of gangs and gang membership?

■ Read Genesis 45:3-20 and 50:15-21. God ultimately uses the actions of Joseph's brothers for good. In what ways have you seen God turn gang activity into something good?

After the discussion, think of a number between one and five. Ask each group member to hold up from one to five fingers on one hand. Inform all group members who hold up the number you chose that they are "dead." They now join the other casualties in the "dead zone." (See the activity Bang! You're Dead, below.)

BaNG! YoU'RE DEaD

This activity should be continued throughout a session on gang violence. At some point during the first activity, interrupt the conversation to ask for a couple of volunteers. When two group members have volunteered, say to them, "Bang! You're dead." These "dead gang members" must sit together in a designated corner of the room, called the "dead zone," to observe, but not participate in, one or more activities. Then continue with the activity.

GaNG CHOiCE

If you conducted the activity Bang! You're Dead (p. 24), invite the "dead gang members" to tell about their experience in the "dead zone." Ask:

■ What truth about gangs is illustrated by this activity?

Reflect together, silently or aloud, on this quote by Martin Luther King, Jr.: *We must learn to live as brothers or we will perish together as fools.*

THe GREaT REVeRSE

Distribute **Bibles** and explain: In this story, told by Jesus, we hear about someone whom Jesus' listeners would have considered "out," an outcast to be avoided at all costs. Listen for that character identified as a Samaritan. Also in this story are two people, a priest and a Levite, whom Jesus' listeners would have assumed were definitely "in." Try to decide what Jesus is saying about who is really "in." Ask a volunteer to read aloud Luke 10:30-37. Discuss:

■ Considering how Jesus' listeners felt about Samaritans, what do you think Jesus was saying to them?

■ Who are the "Samaritans" at your school? What might Jesus be saying to you about them?

■ When have we felt like "Samaritans" at school? What is Jesus saying about us at these times?

■ Considering how Jesus' listeners felt about priests and Levites, what do you think Jesus was saying to them?

■ Who are the "priests" and "Levites" at your school? What might Jesus be saying to you about them?

■ When have we taken the role of "priests" and "Levites" at school? What is Jesus saying about us at these times?

FaSHiON FASCiSTS

On **chalkboard or newsprint** draw a large chart with three columns. Title the columns *Society Says, God Says* and *We say.* Ask:

■ What are some of the messages society gives us about personal appearance? What do you see in advertisements? music videos? movies? *Examples:* I'll be happy if people think I'm sexy. Only thin women and muscular guys have value.

Write answers in the first column of the chart. After group members have listed about a dozen statements, read aloud 1 Samuel 16:7 and ask:

■ What do you think God's answer would be to each of these statements? (Record in second column.)

Finally, ask group members to respond to the statements in the first two columns:

■ What's wrong with the statements in the first column?

■ To what extent can we believe and live by the statements in the second column?

Moral Choices

WHeRE TO Go?

Copy this list on **chalkboard or newsprint**:

parent	teacher	school counselor
peer friend	pastor	adult friend
God	myself	youth leader
brother/sister	magazine	Bible
celebrity model	other	

Then distribute **paper** and **pencils**. Invite group members to reflect: Who would you rely on if you needed help to make a moral decision? Rewrite the list in the order you would choose.

Invite group members to call out their top five choices for moral guidance. Ask:

■ Why did you rank these people first?

■ What would you hope to get from them?

■ How might the order change depending on the situation?

THe SeLLiNG oF SeX

Distribute **magazines, poster board, scissors, glue** and **markers**. Divide into groups of 3-4. Offer the following instructions: With the members of your small group, look through the magazines for examples of how our culture views sex. (*Examples*: advertisements that use sex to sell something, articles that reveal contemporary attitudes toward sex, etc.) Talk together about what your discoveries tell you about sex. Cut out several of the advertisements or article titles that you find and glue them to the poster board. Add titles or captions. Let your poster reflect the messages you see and hear about sex.

After groups complete their posters, let them explain them to the other groups. Then ask:

■ What messages about sex do we receive from our culture?

■ With which of these messages do we agree? Why? With which do we disagree? Why?

BeYoND THe BoDY

Distribute **Bibles** and invite a volunteer to read aloud 1 Corinthians 6:15-17. Ask:

■ According to these verses, what happens in sex?

■ What change takes place when two people have sex?

■ What do you think "becoming one" means mentally? emotionally? spiritually?

Ask another volunteer to read aloud 1 Corinthians 6:18-20. Discuss:

■ God never sets guidelines to restrict or limit us. God's guidelines ultimately lead to our happiness. What do you think these verses mean when they say that the misuse of sex damages us?

■ When it comes to sex and dating, how can we use our bodies "for God's glory"?

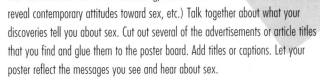

Moral Choices

27

GoSSiP HaLT

Divide participants into smaller groups of 3-4 members each. Distribute **Bibles, paper** and **pencils**. Give the following instructions, pausing between each to allow time for the groups to work:

- Read James 3:1-6 aloud in your small group.
- In verses 1-6, James compares the tongue to three things: a small bit, a small rudder and a tiny flame. What do all these images have in common?
- With your group, think up another one or two images that communicate the same idea about the tongue: how something very small can have a huge effect well beyond its size.
- Now read James 3:7-12.
- When have you seen the tongue used for great good? When have you seen the tongue used for great evil?
- When have you seen the tongue used for giving thanks to God? When have you seen the tongue used for cursing other people?

When groups have finished their discussions, regather and discuss:

- What new images did your group invent to show the power of the tongue?
- What examples of the power of the tongue did your group think of?

THe GoSSiP TRaP

Recruit 8 volunteers and ask them to stand in a line in the center of the group. Hand the first person in line a **pencil** and a **pad of paper**. Offer these instructions to the volunteers:

- The first person in the line writes on the pad a simple sentence describing something positive and true about the eighth and final person in the line. The sentence should be no more than 10 words long, for example: Kai works out three days a week at home.
- The first person then passes the pad to the second person in the line, who changes just one word in the sentence on the pad.
- Play continues down the line, with volunteers 3 through 7 each changing just one word in the sentence.
- When the pad gets to the final person in line, he or she reads it aloud. At this point, volunteer 8 steps to the front of the line and confronts the first volunteer on the final form of what is written on the pad, saying, for example, "I heard you said this. What's going on?"
- The final volunteer moves down the line of volunteers, finding out how, where and why the story changed, setting the record straight and "clearing his or her name."

LYiNG AROuND

Before your meeting recruit a quick-thinking volunteer to take the role of a *compulsive liar*. Prepare the liar by explaining:

- Your job will be to answer all questions with lies.
- The "truth" that you are trying to hide is this: There is a fire starting in the next room of the building.
- It will be the group's job to get this "truth" out of you.

In your meeting, introduce your volunteer with these explanations:

- This is *(name of volunteer)*. She (or he) is a compulsive liar. Nothing she (or he) says is the truth.
- She (or he) knows something extremely important for us to know. We've got to get it out of her (or him).
- I'll begin by asking the first question: "Is there an emergency somewhere?"

When the group has either figured out the emergency or given up in frustration, continue with activity I Never Lie (next column).

I NeVER LiE!

Begin with the activity Lying Around (previous column). Then ask:

- What problems were caused by the volunteer's lies?

Distribute **pencils** and **paper**. Read aloud the following Truth and Lie Inventory and ask group members to write a T or F after each statement. Ask group members to put their names somewhere on the backs of their papers. When group members have finished, collect their papers and tally the scores for each item on the inventory. Return members' papers and read the results of the inventory, item by item. Allow time for discussion after each item. You could ask:

- Are you surprised by our answers to this item? Explain.
- What do we learn about ourselves from our answers to this question?
- Was it difficult or easy to answer this question? Explain.

THE TRUTH AND LIE INVENTORY

- I never lie.
- I rarely lie.
- I lie, but I feel bad about it afterward.
- I lie to protect myself.
- I lie to protect others.
- I never lie to my friends.
- Sometimes it's okay to lie.
- Everyone lies.
- I know at least one person who never lies.
- Jesus never lied.
- There are sometimes good reasons for lying.
- God wants us to tell the truth always.
- God knows that an occasional lie is necessary.
- Telling the truth always brings positive results.
- Telling the truth is a way of trusting God.
- I feel better about myself when I am honest, even if it causes trouble.

SHOPPiNG YOuR WaY TO JAiL

Distribute **paper** and **pencils** and invite group members to write answers to these questions (*without* putting their names on the papers):

■ How often have you shoplifted in the last year?

■ If you have shoplifted in the last year, what did you steal?

■ If you shoplifted in the last year, what was your reason for shoplifting?

■ Do you believe shoplifting is wrong? If so, why? If not, why not?

Ask two volunteers to collect the papers and to summarize the answers on **chalkboard or newsprint**, guarding confidentiality. Discuss:

■ Are the results of our poll surprising? not surprising?

■ How would you feel about shoplifting if you were the owner of a small store? the parent of someone who shoplifted? the child of someone who shoplifted?

■ Why do people shoplift? Share the information in Shoplifting Incentives. Which motives fit your experience? What other motives would you add to the list?

■ How would you help someone overcome a problem with shoplifting?

SHOPLIFTING INCENTIVES

#1 Shoplifting is a way to get recognized, to surprise and impress friends.

#2 Shoplifting—and getting caught—is a way to get attention. Sometimes negative attention is better than no attention at all.

#3 Shoplifters may feel cheated because others have more material possessions, or they may come from families that can't afford some basic necessities.

#4 Stealing can fill emotional needs. The acquisition of "stuff" can temporarily satisfy emotional cravings. Shoplifting can work the way shopping does for many adults.

#5 Shoplifting can be an expression of anger, a way to strike out against authority and social standards.

#6 Shoplifting may be a response to peer pressure. Members of a social group can insist that you prove yourself by breaking the rules.

#7 Poor role models can contribute to shoplifting. Teenagers whose parents nonchalantly steal from their companies or cheat on their taxes teach their kids that taking what belongs to others is okay.

WHY GOSSiP?

Begin with the activity The Gossip Trap (p. 28). Then invite group members to discuss the game:

- What happened to the message passed down the line?
- What does the game illustrate about how a story about someone changes as it's passed from person to person?
- Relate a time when something that was true about you became twisted as people passed it along.
- What is gossip? How do we recognize gossip? What different forms does gossip take?
- Why do people gossip? What does gossip do for those who gossip? What do we have to lose if we stop gossiping?
- What's the result of gossip? What can result for the one who gossips? for the one who is gossiped about?
- At what point does sharing information become gossip?

YeS oR No?

Distribute **Bibles** and ask for five volunteers to read 1 Samuel 26 dramatically. Assign these roles: narrator, David, Abishai, Abner and Saul. After the reading, discuss:

- Imagine that you are Abishai, trying to convince David to kill Saul. What reasons do you give?
- Imagine that you are God, trying to convince David to spare Saul. What reasons do you give?
- Imagine that you are David, unsure of the right thing to do. What are you feeling? thinking? What experiences or beliefs do you draw on to make a decision?
- What difficult moral choices do you and your friends face at school? with friends? with girl-friends or boyfriends? with parents? at work?
- What gives you direction and strength to do the right thing?

BuT, HONeSTLY...

Distribute **paper** and **pencils.** Invite group members to respond in writing to the following questions. Pause for reflection after each question:

- Describe things that people have stolen from you. These things may be tangible, like money, books or in-line skates, or intangible, like relationships, peace of mind or self-respect.
- Describe how you responded when someone stole from you. How did you feel? What did you think about? How did you handle it?
- Describe a time when you stole from someone else. Why did you do it?
- Describe the effect your stealing had on the other person. Describe the effect your stealing had on you.

When members have finished, regather and invite volunteers to share their answers and insights.

31

TRuTH oR ConSeQueNCeS

Distribute **Bibles** and invite group members to turn to Genesis 20. Recruit volunteers to read aloud this passage, each volunteer reading one paragraph. After the reading, divide participants into smaller groups of 3-4 members each. Ask group members to identify all of the consequences of Abraham and Sarah's lie and then to think of a similar contemporary situation, in which one person's lie to protect him- or herself causes grief for many people. Give groups 5-10 minutes to complete their discussions, then regather and discuss:

- Why did Abraham lie?
- What were the consequences of Abraham's lie?
- Share your group's contemporary version of the story from Genesis.
- What is the initial lie?
- Who suffers because of the lie?
- What does it take to "undo" the lie's damage?

CHeATeRS ANONYMOuS

Bring to your meeting a variety of **familiar games**, such as Monopoly, Uno, Yahtzee, Parcheesi, Life, etc. Bring one per every four group members. Divide into groups of four and let each group choose a game. Then give these instructions: We have one new rule for our games today: Cheating is not only allowed, it's expected. But as in a regular game, if you're caught cheating, you're out of the game.

Play the games for 15-20 minutes. Whoever is ahead (and still in the game) at that point is the winner for each game. Discuss:

- How did you feel, cheating?
- What did you gain from cheating?
- Was it easy or difficult to cheat? Explain.
- How many of us got caught cheating? How did we feel when we got caught?
- Who among us chose not to cheat? Why? How did you feel not cheating? What did you gain from not cheating?
- How many of us who won think we won because we cheated?

MaNY FaCeS OF DeCEPTioN

Divide into groups of three or four members. Then give these instructions: It's easy to identify some obvious ways of cheating, stealing and lying. But there are many subtler ways in which people lie, cheat or steal as well. With your group, brainstorm some of life's less obvious ways to deceive. Then prepare two or more quick roleplays that illustrate those ways.

Give groups about 10 minutes to discuss and prepare their roleplays. If necessary, offer these examples to groups:

- An athlete using steroids.
- A food manufacturer using inferior or spoiled ingredients.
- A restaurant serving smaller portions than pictured on the menu.

When groups are ready, invite each group to present its roleplays. After each roleplay, discuss:

- Who was deceiving and how in this roleplay?
- Do you agree that this was deception? Why or why not?
- What was the result of lying, cheating or stealing in this roleplay? What further results could have been shown?
- What would have been the result if no one had deceived another?

JuST SaY SToP!

Distribute **Bibles** and invite group members to turn together to Ephesians 4:28. Ask a volunteer to read this verse aloud. Discuss:

- When it comes to stealing, Paul (the author of this letter) says, "Stop!"
- But Paul doesn't leave it at that. He mentions three *positive* things to do instead. What are they?
- Recall things that people have taken from us. If those who stole from us could instead have done something positive for us, what might they have done?
- Think back to some of the things we have taken from others. If we replaced those items with something positive done for those from whom we stole, what would we do?

GOaL CaRDS

Distribute **index cards** and **pencils**. Invite group members to write down a plan for making a moral decision during the coming week. Then gather in a circle and pray by finishing this sentence:

- Lord, help me to make the right decision about...

Friendship Skills

FRIENDSHIP SKILLS

GeTTiNG iT WRoNG!

Begin a session on friendship skills by giving examples of *terrible* friendship skills. Invite two volunteers to stand in front of the group. Explain:

- ◼ I'd like one of you to share a problem; at this point it's best not share a real problem, *because...*
- ◼ ...the other person will respond in the worst possible way...neither listening, nor supporting.

- ◼ In other words, demonstrate what *not* to say when someone shares a problem.

Repeat the activity several times with different volunteers. Ask:

- ◼ What's wrong with the responses we're hearing?
- ◼ What are we learning about how *not* to help a friend with a problem?

34

GoD-LiSTeNiNG

Distribute **Bibles** and invite group members to turn together to Luke 11:5-13. Invite a volunteer to read aloud Luke 11:5-8. Discuss:

- What kind of listener is the friend in Jesus' story? What motivates his "generosity"?
- When has someone "listened" to you in this way, more to get rid of you than because of true caring?

Ask another volunteer to read aloud Luke 11:9-10. Discuss:

- In contrast to the friend in Jesus' story, these verses describe the way *God* listens. What happens when we ask something of God? seek after God? "knock" at God's door?
- How do we know when God has listened to our asking, seeking or knocking?

Ask a third volunteer to read aloud Luke 11:11-13. Discuss:

- Think of modern versions of Jesus' examples in verses 11-12. For example, "Would any of you give your children paint thinner when they ask for a drink?"
- If human parents listen lovingly to their children, how much more will God! According to Jesus, what kind of listener is God?

JOiNT DiSCoVeRY

Distribute **Bibles** and invite volunteers to read aloud Exodus 18:1-12, each volunteer reading a verse or two. Discuss:

- In these verses, Jethro is laying the groundwork for helping Moses with a major problem. That problem—and its solution—is described in verses 13-27. But here—in verses 1-12—before the problem is even stated, how does Jethro show his support of Moses?
- How can we show our support for friends, day by day, support that would make it possible for us to help them solve a problem later on?

Invite volunteers to read aloud Exodus 18:13-27, each volunteer reading a verse or two. Discuss:

- What questions does Jethro ask to help Moses open up about his problem?
- What fresh perspective on Moses' problem does Jethro give to Moses?
- How does Moses respond to Jethro's advice? What is the result?
- When has someone given you new insight into a personal problem, just by asking the right questions?

Friendship Skills

LEaDeRSHiP SKiLLS

Divide into groups of five. Review the list of Listening Tools on this page. Then offer these instructions:

■ Choose two of the members of your group to roleplay two friends discussing a problem, one the *helper* and the other the *helpee*.

■ The discussion starts with the *helpee* making this statement: *I can't believe I failed another test in that class. There's no point in even trying.*

■ It's the job of the remaining three members of your group to suggest to the *helper* ways to keep that conversation going. Use the Listening Tools you have reviewed.

After several minutes, ask each group to choose a new *helper* and new *helpee* and to repeat the activity using a problem suggested by the group's new *helpee*.

LISTENING TOOLS

■ *Open-Ended Questions:*
Yes or no questions tend to shut conversation down, while open-ended questions invite feelings and complex thoughts. Here are two good ways to start open-ended questions: "How do you feel about..." and "What do you think about..."

■ *Summary Statements:*
Summary statements help to clarify what a person is feeling, thinking or needing. After making the statement, ask if what you've just summarized is correct.

■ *Next-Step Questions:*
A next-step question asks what the person will do about the problem. This shouldn't sound like an interrogation, but a discussion about different ways to handle it. Don't criticize any plan, but help the person explore options. People feel less stress when they know they have choices.

■ *Action Reflection:*
Summarize the options and encourage the person to choose the best action. Talk about what's been done already and what needs to be done next. Action reflection helps lead the person to do something about the problem.

GROuP PRaYERS

Divide into groups of three. Invite participants each to pray for the person on his or her left. Allow several minutes for prayer, then ask participants to gather in a circle. Close by praying:

■ God, help us to understand our problems. Help us to know what's happening, to acknowledge how we feel, to say what we want and to see our options. *Amen.*

IT'S TiME!

Distribute **Bibles** and turn to Ecclesiastes 3:1-14. Divide into two groups; read verse 1 in unison, then read verses 2-8 responsively by dividing each line into two parts, one group reading the first part of each line, the other group the second:

- *first group:* He sets the time for birth...
- *second group:* ...and the time for death...

After finishing verse 8, discuss:

- What do you think is the overall point of these verses?
- Which verses can you relate specifically to relationships?

While some of the verse have obvious meaning for relationships, challenge group members to go further; for example:

- In friendship, when is there a time to "find"? a time to "lose" or let go?
- In families, when is the time for "tearing"? for "mending"?

Ask group members to read silently the remaining portion of the reading, verses 9-14. Ask:

- When facing ever-changing relationships, what advice can we find in these verses? what comfort?

ToNS 'O ReLATiONSHiPS

Before the meeting, prepare role slips by copying each of these roles on a separate **slip of paper**:

- whiny friend at school
- coach upset because student isn't committed enough
- strict mother or father
- supportive best friend
- younger sibling who looks up to student
- bullying older sister or brother
- favorite teacher who likes this student a lot
- teacher who doesn't respect student
- ex-girlfriend or ex-boyfriend carrying a grudge
- demanding girlfriend or boyfriend
- loving grandparent
- worried pastor

Prepare one slip for each participant, *minus 1.*

Recruit one volunteer to play the part of the *student* in a roleplay. Ask all other group members to select a role slip. Give this explanation: The volunteer is a *student*, struggling to handle all the different relationships in life. The rest of us are the different people in the *student's* life. We each have our own special relationship to the *student*, indicated on our slips. And, as we can also see on our slips, we all have different *attitudes* toward the *student*, some positive, some negative. In a moment, we will interact with the *student*, sharing what we're thinking and feeling, and above all, responding to what we've heard the *student* saying to the others of us who share a relationship with the *student*. Be as outspoken and creative as you wish.

Invite group members to stand together in a circle. Ask the *student* to move, person by person, around the circle, interacting with each person for 20-30 seconds. As necessary, remind members to stay in their roles.

LeNDiNG SUPPORT

Distribute **pencils** and **paper** and ask group members to write down their responses silently to the following:

■ List five things someone might say to you to support you. *Example: It took courage for you to tell me about this.*

■ List five things someone could do for you to support you. *Example: Let me spend time with them, just sitting quietly.*

When group members have finished, divide into small groups of three or four. Offer the following instructions: In your group, choose one person to be the first *helpee*. The helpee briefly describes a personal problem. Then each group member gives a possible "supporting" response, one that offers acceptance, provides strength or lends protection. Use the ideas for supportive statements that you wrote down earlier. After all responses have been offered, the helpee will tell which comments from group members felt most supportive and why. Give each member of the group a chance to be the helpee.

CHaLLeNGiNG

Invite group members to discuss:

■ Think of your best friend, the person to whom you feel closer than any other in the world.

■ Now, without saying it aloud, think about what makes that person so important to you.

■ Now, again silently, think about a time when you confronted that person about something, or a time when that person confronted you.

After about 30 seconds, invite volunteers each to share one time of confrontation they've experienced with someone to whom they feel close. Discuss:

■ What makes challenging difficult?

■ When is challenging the right thing to do? How do we decide?
— What sorts of things do we believe call for challenging?
— When is challenging or confronting someone a responsibility?

■ What are some good ways to challenge?

■ What should we avoid when challenging?

■ If you were messing up and needed to be challenged, how could it be done most effectively? What would work with you? What would you want your challenging friend to say?

■ In your life right now, who would have the "right" to challenge you?

SORTING OuT

Begin with the activity Tons 'O Relationships (p. 37). Then invite the *student* to discuss his or her role:

■ To what extent did this feel like real life?

■ Describe your feelings as you went further around the circle. Did you feel pressured? overwhelmed? annoyed? frustrated?

■ To what extent did your role as the *student* get more complicated as you went around the circle?

Ask the other members to discuss their roles in the activity:

■ To what extent did this mirror what happens in all our lives? How often do we feel the pressure of competing relationships? of changing relationships?

■ How did the *student* change as he (or she) proceeded around the circle? How did his (or her) responses change? his (or her) attitude?

Ask all groups members:

■ In what ways do changing relationships bring change to our lives?

■ What changes have relationships brought to your family? to your life at school? to other friendships?

■ How have your relationships changed how you feel about yourself? about God?

NoT BaCKiNG DoWN

Distribute **Bibles** and invite participants to find Acts 10:9-23. Read this aloud. Then discuss:

■ What's Peter's problem in these verses?

■ In what ways does God challenge Peter?

— What's the challenge for Peter in the vision of verses 11-13?

— What's the challenge for Peter in the voice of the Spirit in verses 19-20?

■ How does Peter respond to God's challenge?

After your discussion, divide into groups of three or four and offer these instructions: Plan and practice a brief reenactment of Peter's story, only in a contemporary setting, for example, in your school or in one of your homes:

■ Replace Peter in the story with one of your group members.

■ Replace Peter's problem in the story with a problem a teenager might face.

■ How might God challenge and change the teenager in your new version of Peter's story?

Invite groups to present their reenactments. When all reenactments have been presented, discuss:

■ In both the original gospel story and in our reenactments, what were the problems that needed confronting?

■ In the gospel story, how did God challenge? What do you think of God's approach?

■ In our reenactments, how did we challenge? What do you think of our approaches?

DeSIGN-a-DaTE

Distribute **index cards** and **pens**. Invite each participant to list the 10 top qualities he or she would like to find in a lasting relationship. Ask them *not* to put their names on their cards.

When everyone has finished, collect, shuffle and redistribute the cards. Ask group members to respond to the following questions with a show of hands:

- How many of you find one or more items on your new card that you also wrote on your card?
- How many find five or more items that you agree with on your new card?
- How many people find only two or fewer items that you agree with?
- How likely do you think you are to find a person like the one described here? like the one described on your original card?
- Which of these qualities do you think are most important in a long-term relationship?

THe FLiP SiDE

Begin with the activity Design-a-Date. Then spread out the index cards on a table and ask group members to retrieve their original cards. Give these instructions: Silently reread the items on your card. As you read each item, consider: What in me would attract someone with this quality?

After 2 minutes of silence, continue: We've talked a lot about what we'd like to see in a potential steady date. Now silently ask yourself what you can bring to a relationship that would make it lasting. What would you offer to a potential boyfriend or girlfriend?

Pause for 2 more minutes of silence, then ask volunteers to share their thoughts.

40

FELLoWSHiP CHaLLeNGE

Offer these instructions: Sometime this week, call one other person in this group and just talk with him or her for a few minutes. Consider choosing someone you don't know very well. Ask how the person is doing and what he or she has been going through.

MYTHS aND MiSCoNCePTioNS

Copy the questions below onto **chalkboard or newsprint**. Then divide into pairs and invite each pair to pick one of the questions to discuss.

■ How does what we look for in friends differ from what we look for in someone to date?

■ From your own experience, name the biggest misconception you think people have about dating.

■ What gives a person the power to say, "I'm not ready to date" or "I'm not interested in dating right now"?

■ What's the best and worst thing about dating?

Give partners 3-5 minutes, then ask each pair to join with another pair to form a group of four. Give these instructions: Share with your new group one insight you gained in your pair. Then pick one new question to discuss in your group of four. Give groups 5-10 minutes, then ask each group of four to join with another group of four. Give the same instructions. After 10 minutes, regather the large group.

Ask:

■ What myths or misconceptions about dating did your pairs or groups identify?

■ What was the best thing you heard about dating?

QUiCK QUaLiTiES

Invite group members to sit in a large circle. Stand in the middle of the circle and explain: In a moment I am going to say an incomplete statement. I will then point to someone in the circle. If I point to you, immediately repeat the statement, completing it with the first word or phrase that pops into your head. Then the next person clockwise in the circle will complete the statement with their own word or phrase. We will move clockwise around the circle, repeating and completing the statement. Speed is important; move as quickly as you can. Remember, say the first thing that comes to mind. Here's the statement: When it comes to steady dating, my ideal person would be...

Loneliness & Jealousy

BEHiND THe FaCeS

Before the meeting prepare **slips of paper on which you have written roles**. Write one role on each sheet. Suggested roles include: beauty queen, jock, rebel, nerd, Casanova/playboy, flirt, smart Einstein type, someone with AIDS, politician, homeless person, wealthy person, druggie, elderly person, musician, Hare Krishna, drug dealer, prostitute, ex-convict, physically challenged person, etc. Add other roles of your own and feel free to repeat roles, if necessary, to be sure you have prepared one role for each participant.

As each group member arrives, **pin** to his or her back one of the role slips prepared before the meeting. Be certain that members do not see the roles being pinned to their backs. Give these instructions: Treat each person in the group according to his or her role. Try to guess from the way people treat you what is written on your back.

Continue with the activity Face Confessions (p. 43).

JeSUS ALoNE

Ask:

- When do you think Jesus felt the loneliest?
- When do we feel lonely?
- When do our parents experience loneliness? our teachers? our friends?
- In what ways can we overcome loneliness?
- How can Jesus help us?
  — What example did Jesus set for us in the garden of Gethsemane (Mark 14:32-36)?
  — Who is present with us, even when family and friends are not?

Distribute **paper** and **pencils** and invite group members to write prayers that ask God for help in overcoming loneliness.

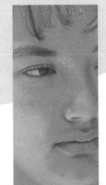

FaCe CoNFeSSioNS

After you have completed the activity Behind the Faces (p. 42), discuss:

- In this game, who felt liked? accepted? popular? How were these people treated?
- Who felt lonely? shunned? unaccepted? unpopular? How were these people treated?
- When in our day-to-day lives do we feel the most lonely?
- What's the difference between being alone and feeling lonely?
- When is being alone okay? When does being alone feel lonely?
- When do we feel lonely, even in a group?
- Why do people experience loneliness?
- Respond to this statement: *Everyone experiences loneliness.* To what degree is this statement true?

ENCOuRAGiNG THe LONeLY

Ask a volunteer to sit in the center of the group circle. Invite the volunteer to complete this statement: *I feel loneliest when...*

After the volunteer has completed the statement, give each group member an opportunity to respond to the volunteer's completed statement with a way to cope with the lonely situation named by the volunteer. Repeat with other volunteers.

No ONe LoNeLY

Complete the activity called All the Lonely (below). Then invite participants to return to their small groups, read John 20:11-18, and make a list of all the different feelings Mary probably experienced in verses 11b-18. Then regather and ask:

■ Now what do you imagine Mary is feeling? Add these feelings to your chalkboard list.

■ What has changed the way Mary feels?

■ How can the knowledge that Jesus is alive and with us help us deal with our own feelings of loneliness?

QUiCK SuRVeY

Invite group members to stand in a circle. Ask each group member to complete this statement, quickly and without much thought: *I tend to be jealous of...*

Continue with these statements, letting all group members respond before starting a new statement:

■ People tend to be jealous of my...

■ Jealousy is...

■ Jealousy hurts because...

ALL THe LoNeLY

Distribute **pencils, Bibles** and **paper.** Divide participants into groups of 4-5 members each and ask each small group to read together John 20:1-11a, stopping at the line that reads, "Mary stood crying outside the tomb." Then have group members make a list of all the different feelings Mary probably experienced as she spent this time in the garden. What was she feeling in verses 1-11a? Give groups time to complete their reading and their lists, then gather and ask:

■ What feelings did you list? Record responses on **chalkboard or newsprint**.

■ Which of the feelings we've just listed are a part of loneliness?

■ When have you felt the kind of loneliness Mary feels in these verses?

PiCTURiNG JeaLOuSY

Distribute **drawing paper** and **colored felt markers**. Invite each group member to draw a picture of jealousy. Say:

- What does jealousy look like? feel like? See if you can capture the look and feel of jealousy in your picture.
- Your picture can be literal or symbolic.

Allow 5-10 minutes for drawing, then regather and ask volunteers to show and explain their drawings. If you wish, discuss:

- What have we learned about jealousy from our pictures?
- What else would you like to say about jealousy?

JEaLOuS EXCHaNGE

Distribute **paper** and **pencils**. Then ask each group member to write the initials of any 10 people (friends, celebrities, etc.). When lists are complete, ask group members to write beside each name one way in which they are or could be jealous of that particular person. Then ask them to write one way in which each person could be jealous of them. Discuss:

- What is *jealousy*? How does it feel?
- Where does jealousy come from?
- What does jealousy say about how we feel about ourselves? about how we feel about others? about how we feel about God?
- How does jealousy impact our relationships with others?
- How do you think God feels about jealousy?
- What can we do about jealousy? What advice would you give someone who is struggling with jealousy?

Encourage group members to give practical answers to this final question. Write these answers on **chalkboard or newsprint**.

INSTaNT POeTRY

Write the word *JEALOUSY* in large letters on **chalkboard, newsprint or poster board**. Invite group members to stand or sit in a circle so all can see the word you've just written. Select a member in the circle. Say to that member, "J is for the..."

That member must immediately complete the statement, *beginning with the letter J and making a statement about jealousy.* For example:

■ **J** is for the...Joy we lose because of jealousy.

Select another member in the circle and say to that member, "E is for the..." (Sample answer: **E** is for...the End of friendships.)

Continue for the remaining letters of the word *jealousy:*

■ **A** is for...Always feeling inferior.

■ **L** is for...Losing all peace of mind.

■ etc.

I'M JEaLOuS!

Give those group members who are first to arrive at the meeting several **cookies** with these instructions: Wait to eat your cookies until other group members have arrived. Don't share your cookies; you must eat them all yourselves. As other group members arrive—those without cookies—try to make them jealous of you and your cookies. Say things like: Mmm, these are good. We got cookies—you didn't! I wonder why? Don't you wish you had gotten some cookies?

Let this continue until all group members have settled in the room and all the cookies have been eaten. Then discuss:

■ What do you think is going on here?

■ How were those with cookies acting?

■ How did those of you who didn't get cookies feel when you saw what was happening? How many were, to at least a small degree, jealous? Why?

THE POISON OF JEALOUSY

Distribute **Bibles** and invite group members to find Numbers 12:1-16. Explain that the characters in this story—Miriam, Aaron and Moses—are siblings. Read Numbers 12:1-16 dramatically, assigning the parts of the narrator, Miriam, Aaron and Moses. Then discuss:

■ Of what are Miriam and Aaron jealous? When has jealousy surfaced in your family? among your friends?

■ What is God's *verbal* response to Miriam and Aaron?

■ What's the *physical* consequence of Miriam and Aaron's jealousy? How can jealousy bring its own negative consequences? What has resulted from jealousy in your family? among your friends?

■ In the end, Miriam is healed. How are we healed of the damage brought by jealousy?

WHAT I'VE GOT!

Distribute **paper** and **pencils** and ask group members to list at least five things about themselves that they could appreciate the next time they're tempted to be jealous of someone else.

After everyone has finished, give each group member a chance to affirm something about him- or herself by completing either of these statements:

■ I really appreciate my...

■ I really appreciate the way I...

JEALOUSY CHARADES

Invite volunteers to pantomime three rounds of "things that make us jealous," as other group members guess what is being pantomimed:

■ First round: group members pantomime *concrete objects* that others own, for example, a car, a nice home, a stereo or a jacket.

■ Second round: group members pantomime *skills or abilities*, for example, the ability to run, sing or get good grades.

■ Third round: group members pantomime *qualities or characteristics*, for example, patience, love, humor or happiness.

Loneliness & Jealousy